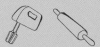

Holiday Cooking for Kids!

EASTER
Sweets and Treats

By Ruth Owen

WINDMILL
BOOKS

New York

Published in 2013 by Windmill Books, An Imprint of Rosen Publishing
29 East 21st Street, New York, NY 10010

First Edition

Produced for Windmill by Ruby Tuesday Books Ltd
Editor for Ruby Tuesday Books Ltd: Mark J. Sachner
US Editor: Sara Antill
Designer: Trudi Webb

Library of Congress Cataloging-in-Publication Data

Owen, Ruth, 1967–
 Easter sweets and treats / by Ruth Owen.
   p. cm. — (Holiday cooking for kids!)
 Includes index.
 ISBN 978-1-4488-8084-3 (library binding) — ISBN 978-1-4488-8131-4 (pbk.) —
ISBN 978-1-4488-8137-6 (6-pack)
 1. Easter cooking—Juvenile literature. 2. Desserts—Juvenile literature. I. Title.
 TX739.2.E37O94 2013
 641.5'68—dc23

                    2012009781

Manufactured in the United States of America

CPSIA Compliance Information: Batch # B3S12WM: For Further Information contact Windmill Books, New York, New York at 1-866-478-0556

Contents

A Festival of Rebirth and Renewal

Easter is **one of the most holy days** on the Christian calendar. It marks the end of Lent, a period of **fasting**, prayer, and **self-reflection** that lasts about 40 days. The last week of Lent is called Holy Week and contains Good Friday, which marks the **crucifixion** and death of Jesus. According to the Christian Bible, Jesus rose from the dead on the third day after his crucifixion. His **resurrection** is celebrated on Easter Sunday.

The date on which Easter is celebrated changes every year. Generally, it falls between March 22 and April 25. Historically, its date has been based on several factors, including the date of the Jewish Passover and the first full moon of spring.

Easter is a time to celebrate both rebirth in nature and, for Christians, the resurrection of Jesus. It's also a time for feasting and giving treats, such as candy Easter eggs and their junior cousins, jelly beans!

The recipes in this book will give you some great Easter treats to give as gifts, and for sharing at Easter get-togethers with family and friends.

Before you start cooking, check out all the tips and information on the following pages.

Before You Begin Cooking

Get Ready to Cook

- Wash your hands using soap and hot water. This will help to keep bacteria away from your food.
- Make sure the kitchen countertop and all your equipment is clean.
- Read the recipe carefully before you start cooking. If you don't understand a step, ask an adult to help you.
- Gather all the ingredients and equipment you will need.

Safety First!

It's very, very important to have an adult around whenever you do any of the following tasks in the kitchen:

1. Operating machinery or turning on kitchen appliances such as a mixer, food processor, blender, stovetop burners, or the oven.

2. Using sharp utensils, such as knives, can openers, or vegetable peelers.

3. Working with hot pots, pans, or cookie sheets.

Cake tin

Mixing bowl

Saucepan

Frying pan

Rolling pin

Cutting board

Knif

Wooden spoon

You will need these kitchen utensils to make the recipes in this book.

Sieve

Electric hand mixer

Oven mitt

Cupcake pan

Grater

Whisk

Vegetable peeler

Cookie sheet

Measuring Counts!

Measure your ingredients carefully. If you get a measurement wrong, it could affect how successful your dish turns out to be. Measuring cups and spoons are two of the most important pieces of equipment in a kitchen.

Measuring cup

Measuring Cups

Measuring cups are used to measure the volume, or amount, of liquid or dry ingredients. Measuring cups usually hold from 1 cup to 4 cups. If you have a 1-cup measuring cup, that should be fine for all the recipes in this book. Measuring cups have markings on them that show how many cups or parts of a cup you are measuring.

Measuring Spoons

Like measuring cups, measuring spoons are used to measure the volume of liquid or dry ingredients, only in smaller amounts. Measuring spoons come in sets with different spoons for teaspoons, tablespoons, and smaller parts.

Measuring spoons

Cooking Techniques

Here are some tasks that anyone who is following directions for cooking should be sure to understand.

Bringing to a boil

Heating a liquid or mixture in a saucepan on the stovetop until it is bubbling.

Simmering

First bringing a liquid or mixture to a boil, and then turning down the heat so it's just at or below the boiling point and the bubbling has nearly stopped.

Preheating

Heating the oven until it has reached the temperature required for the recipe.

All of these tasks require the use of heat, so you should be absolutely sure to have an adult around when you do them.

Easter Brunch Eggs

Easter and eggs. It's a connection that reminds us that Easter is both a holy feast day and a **celebration** of spring. Eggs and newly hatched chicks **symbolize** the start of a new life in nature, just as spring welcomes the rebirth of life out of the ground. For Christians, the promise of a new life coming from an egg is also a reminder of the resurrection of Jesus from the tomb. Here is a recipe that you can prepare for an Easter breakfast or brunch. It's fun to make and reminds us of one of Easter's most beloved symbols, the egg.

You will need – ingredients:

Serves six people, or three people with two eggs each!

6 large eggs

1 tablespoon milk or half-and-half

¼ teaspoon salt

⅛ teaspoon ground black pepper

2 tablespoons butter

1 tablespoon chopped chives

Toast, English muffins, or other type of toasted bread

You will need – equipment:

Knife

2 medium mixing bowls

Hand whisk or fork

Frying pan

Wooden spoon or spatula

Sugar spoon

6 eggcups or other type of cups or miniature drinking glasses small enough to hold an egg

Step-by-Step:

1. Carefully crack the tops off the eggs with a sharp knife. Pour out the eggs into a bowl.

2. Rinse out the eggshells well with hot water and set aside.

3. Add the salt and pepper and the milk or half-and-half to the eggs and whisk well.

4. Gently melt the butter in the frying pan over a medium heat. Be sure the butter doesn't turn brown.

5. Add the egg mixture and cook, stirring constantly with the wooden spoon or spatula, until the eggs begin to thicken. Be careful not to let the eggs burn on the pan, and stir so that the liquid and solid parts blend together until there is no liquid in the pan.

6. Using the wooden spoon or spatula, remove the eggs from the frying pan into a clean mixing bowl.

7. Mix the chopped chives into the scrambled egg.

8. Using a sugar spoon, gently scoop portions of scrambled egg into the empty eggshells.

9. Place in eggcups or some other kind of cup or glass that is narrow enough to hold the eggs.

10. Serve with buttered toast.

Safety Tips for Preparing Scrambled Eggs:

Raw, undercooked, or unrefrigerated eggs can be a health hazard. So can eggs that have been sold past their "sell-by" date or that have sat for too long in the fridge. Here are some tips to make sure the eggs you eat are safe:

- Check the "sell-by" date on the cartons of all eggs that you cook and be sure the eggs have been refrigerated properly.

- Be sure the empty eggshells you use have been properly washed out. You may rinse them out with hot water or let them sit in boiling water for a few minutes and then carefully remove them with a large spoon and let them drain on some paper towel off to the side.

- Be sure you wash your hands after handling raw eggs or their shells.

- Be sure to heat the scrambled eggs enough so that there are no signs of liquid remaining in the pan. Remember, scrambled eggs should not be runny eggs!

Easter Bunny Cookies

We all know about the Easter bunny that delivers baskets of colorful eggs to children at Easter. But how did a bunny, and not a bird, come to be delivering eggs?

No one knows for sure, but in ancient times, hares and rabbits were symbols of spring and fertility (the ability to have young) because these animals give birth to large litters of babies in spring. Eggs also symbolized new life and some ancient cultures included eggs in their yearly celebrations of spring and rebirth. Over time, eggs, hares and rabbits, spring, birth, and rebirth became ideas that were entangled. So entangled, in fact, that the myth of an egg-carrying rabbit developed and became a favorite part of Easter!

This Easter make a batch of delicious bunny-shaped cookies and have fun decorating them!

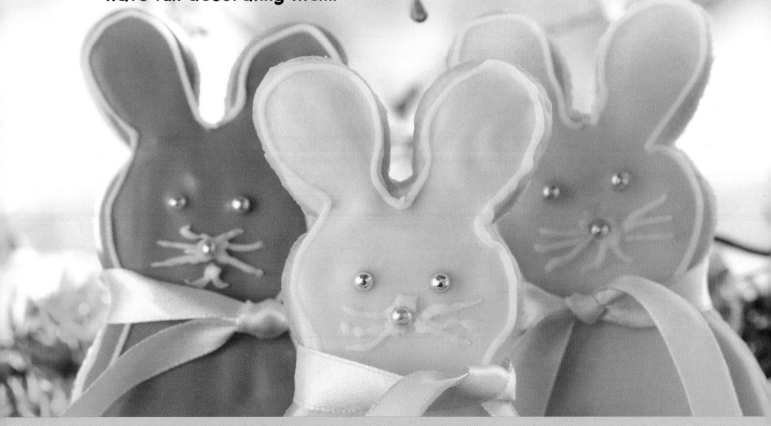

You will need – ingredients:

½ cup (1 stick) butter, softened

¼ cup sugar

1 small egg

1 teaspoon vanilla extract

1½ cups all-purpose flour

teaspoon baking powder

Ready-to-use decorating icing tubes in your choice of colors

Sprinkles or candy for decorating and making faces

Ribbon to tie bows around the bunnies' necks

You will need – equipment:

Large mixing bowl

Electric hand mixer

Plastic wrap

Rolling pin

Clean, flat surface for rolling out dough

Cookie cutter in the shape of an Easter bunny

Cookie sheet

Potholder or oven mitt for handling cookie sheet

Remember to ask an adult for help when you are using the electric hand mixer and oven.

Step-by-Step:

1. Using the electric mixer, beat the butter and sugar together until creamy in the mixing bowl, and then add the egg and vanilla extract and beat until well blended.

2. Gradually add the flour and baking powder, and beat until the dough is just blended.

3. Shape the dough into a ball, wrap in plastic wrap, and cool in the refrigerator for an hour or in the freezer for 30 minutes.

4. Ask an adult to help you preheat the oven to 350°F (175°C).

5. Place the chilled dough on a flat, lightly floured surface and roll out until it's about ¼ inch (6 mm) thick.

6. Cut the Easter bunny shapes out of the dough with your cookie cutter.

Step-by-Step:

7. Place the cookies 1 inch (2.5 cm) apart on the cookie sheet and bake in the preheated oven for 10 to 12 minutes, or until lightly browned. Take out to cool.

8. When the cookies are cool, they're ready to decorate! Use the decorating icing to make the bunnies different colors and to draw their faces. Get creative with sprinkles or candy, too. When the icing is dry, tie a bow around the neck of each cookie bunny.

Carrot Cake

This recipe will produce a delicious, succulent carrot cake with a lemon-flavored frosting that you can serve for dessert after your Easter meal, or enjoy as an afternoon treat.

Carrot cake is wonderfully sweet, but contains lots of healthy carrot goodness. And with all that carrot packed inside, why not save some for the Easter Bunny, because everyone knows that bunnies can't resist carrots!

You will need – ingredients:

To make the carrot cake:

¾ cup dark brown sugar

⅓ pint vegetable oil

4 eggs

1 cup grated carrot

1¼ cups whole-wheat
self-rising flour

1 teaspoon ground cinnamon

1 teaspoon butter (for greasing
cake tin)

To make the frosting:

⅓ cup confectioners'
(powdered) sugar

1 tablespoon butter

1 teaspoon finely grated lemon rind

1 tablespoon lemon juice

Readymade marzipan
carrots to decorate

You will need – equipment:

Vegetable peeler

Grater

Round 8-inch
(20-cm) cake tin

Waxed paper

Scissors

Large mixing bowl

Wooden spoon

Sieve for sifting flour

Potholder or oven mitt for
handling cake tin

Metal skewer

Medium mixing bowl

Butter knife

Step-by-Step:

To make the carrot cake:

1. Ask an adult to help you preheat the oven to 350°F (175°C).

2. Line the cake tin with the waxed paper. You will need to cut slits in the paper to make it fit the tin and cut off excess paper around the top of the tin.

3. Grease the waxed paper with some butter to keep the cake from sticking.

4. Put the sugar and oil into a large mixing bowl, and mix well.

5. Break the eggs into the mixing bowl and beat into the sugar and oil mixture.

6. Stir in the grated carrot.

7. Sieve the flour and cinnamon into the mixture and mix well until all the ingredients are blended.

8. Carefully pour the mixture into the lined cake tin.

9. Bake for 40 minutes. Test to see if the cake is done by inserting a metal skewer into the center. If the skewer comes out clean, the cake is cooked. If not, return to the oven for another 5 to 10 minutes, but check to make sure the top of the cake isn't burning.

10. When the cake is cooked, carefully remove it from the cake tin. Peel off the paper and let the cake cool.

EASTER FOOD FACTS

Carrots are crunchy, delicious, and naturally sweet. They are also good for you. Besides aiding our digestive systems, carrots are a source of beta-carotene, which our bodies turn into **vitamin** A. Vitamin A is essential to many bodily functions, including vision and night vision, especially. So eat carrots and give your body and eyes a boost!

Step-by-Step:

To make the frosting:

1. Put the sugar, butter, grated lemon rind, and lemon juice into a medium mixing bowl.

2. Beat together with the wooden spoon until smooth.

3. When the carrot cake is completely cool, use a butter knife to spread the frosting over the top of the cake and down the sides.

4. Add ready-made carrot decorations, if you'd like, and enjoy!

Easter Nest Cupcakes

Springtime, when Easter falls, is the time of year when many birds are busy building their nests and laying eggs. So it's not surprising that pretty nests that you can eat have become a part of our Easter celebrations. Topped with coconut "grass" and mini chocolate eggs or jelly bean "eggs," these Easter nest cupcakes are easy to bake. You can give them to friends as a delicious homemade Easter gift, or put a cupcake by each place setting at Easter brunch.

You will need – ingredients:

These quantities will make about 10 to 12 cupcakes

1 cup sugar

½ cup butter (1 stick), softened

2 eggs

2 teaspoons vanilla extract

1½ cups all-purpose flour

1¾ teaspoons baking powder

½ cup milk

Ready-made frosting in white, or your favorite color

Shredded coconut

Green food coloring

Bag of jelly beans or mini chocolate eggs

You will need – equipment:

Cupcake pan

Cupcake wrappers

Large mixing bowl

Electric hand mixer

Wooden spoon for stirring

Sieve for sifting flour

Medium mixing bowl

Potholder or oven mitt for handling cupcake pan

Toothpick

Small bowl

Metal spoon

Step-by-Step:

1. Preheat the oven to 350°F (175°C).

2. Line the cupcake pan with the cupcake wrappers.

3. In the large mixing bowl, use the electric mixer to cream together the sugar and butter.

4. One at a time, beat the eggs into the sugar and butter mixture, then stir in the vanilla extract.

5. In the medium bowl, sift together the flour and baking powder.

6. Add the flour mixture to the creamy mixture and mix thoroughly.

7. Add the milk, stirring until the batter is smooth.

8. Pour the batter into the lined cupcake wrappers so that each cup is about $\frac{2}{3}$ full.

9. Bake for 20–25 minutes, until the cupcakes are light brown. Test to see if they're done by sticking a toothpick into the center of a cupcake. If it comes out clean, your cupcakes are ready. Allow the cupcakes to cool.

Step-by-Step:

10. Cover the top of each cupcake with white frosting.

11. Put the shredded coconut into a small bowl. Sprinkle on a few drops of green food coloring and begin to stir with a metal spoon. The coconut will soak up the food coloring. Keep adding drops and stirring until all the coconut "grass" is the shade of green you want.

12. Make a nest of grass on top of each cupcake and add three jellybeans or mini chocolate eggs.

Homemade Easter Eggs

The giving of painted or dyed hens' eggs to celebrate rebirth in spring dates back centuries. The first chocolate Easter eggs weren't made until the early 1800s, though. Chocolate makers in France and Germany created small, solid eggs made from dark, bitter chocolate. Hollow chocolate eggs soon followed, but it was a time-consuming process because they were made from a chocolate paste that had to be spread into the egg-shaped molds by hand.

By the end of the 1800s, chocolate makers had invented a way to process chocolate so that it could be poured into molds, and then set solid. The mass-produced, hollow chocolate eggs we eat today were born!

This Easter make your own chocolate eggs to give to family and friends using this recipe for homemade eggs with a delicious, smooth chocolate filling.

You will need – ingredients:

2½ cups semi sweet chocolate chips

¾ cup heavy cream

Colored foil for wrapping the eggs
(available from craft stores or online)

You will need – equipment:

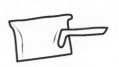

Small saucepan

Hand whisk

Medium mixing bowl

Small bowl

Tablespoon

Cookie sheet

Waxed paper

Wooden spoon

Toothpick

EASTER FOOD FACTS

The chocolate and cream filling used
to fill the homemade Easter eggs in this
recipe was invented in the late 1800s by
chocolate chefs in France and Switzerland.
The delicious, silky mixture is called
ganache. It's the same filling that is used in
the chocolate candies known as truffles.

Step-by-Step:

1. To make the chocolate filling for your Easter eggs, put 1½ cups of chocolate chips into the saucepan with the cream and simmer on the stove at a medium heat.

2. When you see tiny bubbles appear at the edges of the cream, turn off the heat.

3. Let the mixture sit for 3 to 4 minutes while the chocolate melts in the hot cream.

4. Combine the chocolate and cream using the hand whisk. Keep gently whisking until the mixture is smooth and shiny.

5. Pour the mixture into the medium mixing bowl and put into the refrigerator. Let the mixture set solid. This will take at least 2 hours.

6. When the filling is set, it is ready to be made into egg shapes. Using a tablespoon, take a spoonful of filling. Roll it into an egg shape using your fingers. Place the eggs onto a cookie sheet covered with waxed paper.

7. Refrigerate the eggs for another 2 hours.

Step-by-Step:

8. When the eggs are ready to be coated, put the rest of the chocolate chips into a small bowl. Microwave for 30 seconds on high to melt the chocolate.

9. Stir the chocolate using the wooden spoon. Microwave for another 30 seconds, and stir. If you still have lumps, keep stirring and giving the chocolate 10-second blasts in the microwave until it is fully melted and smooth.

10. Using a toothpick, pick up an egg and dip it into the melted chocolate. Make sure the egg is completely coated. Then set the egg onto the cookie sheet. Repeat with all the eggs.

11. Allow the chocolate coating to harden.

12. Wrap each egg in colored foil. Keep your homemade Easter eggs in the refrigerator until you are ready to eat them or give them as gifts.

Deviled Easter Eggs

Jelly beans, chocolate eggs and bunnies, and marshmallow chicks, all gathered together in a grass-lined Easter basket, are a favorite Easter-morning treat. But did you know that the colorful hard-boiled eggs decorating those baskets of goodies can also be turned into a tasty Easter snack called deviled eggs? These eggs get their name because some of the ingredients add a bit of spicy heat!

Use your decorated eggs to make this simple dish, or cook up a batch of hard-boiled eggs as a tasty snack for Easter visitors.

You will need – ingredients:

These ingredients will make enough for 6 to 12 people.

12 eggs

⅓ cup mayonnaise

1 tablespoon yellow or brown mustard

¼ teaspoon salt

⅛ teaspoon ground black pepper

Optional:

1 tablespoon capers

2 tablespoons chopped olives

2 tablespoons chopped pickles

1 teaspoon chopped fresh herbs such as dill, tarragon, thyme, or chives

½ teaspoon curry powder

⅛ teaspoon hot sauce

You will need – equipment:

Large saucepan

Knife

Small mixing bowl

Fork

Sugar spoon

Potholders or oven mitts for handling hot saucepan

Round or oval-shaped platter for serving

Step-by-Step:

Remember to ask an adult for help when you are handling the knife and the stovetop.

1. Place eggs carefully on the bottom of the pot.
    Cover with water about 2 inches (5 cm) above the eggs.

2. Bring to a complete rolling boil on a burner at medium heat. Remove the pot from the heat. Cover the pot and let the eggs sit in the hot water for about 20 minutes.

3. Run cold water into the pot, making sure to run the water long enough so all the water in it is now cold. Leave the eggs in the pot.

4. Making sure your hands are washed, take one egg and carefully smash the shell all around it against the side of the pot. Carefully peel the egg shell off as you hold the egg under cold running water. Place the egg back into the pan of cold water and do the same thing to all the eggs.

5. When all the eggs are peeled, slice each egg in half the long way.

6. Scoop the yolk out of each egg half and put the yolks in a small mixing bowl.

7. Place each sliced egg white hole-side up on a plate. If some of the egg whites seem too broken up to fill, chop them up small and add them to the yolks

8. Add mayonnaise, mustard, salt, and pepper to the yolk mixture and mash it all together with a fork until it is smooth.

Step-by-Step:

9. Add one or more of these ingredients to the egg yolk mixture: capers, chopped olives, chopped pickles, chopped fresh herbs, curry powder, or hot sauce. Make sure it's a flavor you will like. Experiment by mixing a tiny amount of the ingredient with a little of the yolk mix to find out which flavors you prefer.

10. Fill the empty holes in the egg whites with a small mound of yolk mix till all the yolks are used up. Refrigerate until ready to eat, or serve soon at room temperature.

Decorated Eggs to Deviled Eggs

You can peel your decorated hard-boiled eggs and turn them into deviled eggs. It's very important, however, that you follow these hygiene and safety tips:

- If decorated eggs are to be eaten, use food-safe coloring to dye them and wash your hands before handling the eggs.

- Don't eat hard-boiled Easter eggs that have been lying on the ground. Eggs placed on the ground could pick up harmful germs, especially if the shells are cracked. Hide eggs in places where they are unlikely to be contaminated with germs from dirt, moisture, or pets.

- The total time for hiding and hunting eggs should not exceed two hours if you plan to eat the eggs later.

- After being found, eggs must be washed and re-refrigerated, and eaten within seven days of cooking.

Glossary

celebration (seh-luh-BRAY-shun)
Observance of special times, with activities.

crucifixion (kroo-suh-FIK-shun) Putting someone to death by nailing or binding that person by the hands and feet to a cross.

fasting (FAST-ing) Choosing to go without food.

resurrection (reh-zuh-REK-shun) Returning to life from death.

self-reflection (self-rih-FLEK-shun)
Serious thought or meditation about oneself, one's actions, and one's personal or spiritual qualities.

symbolize (SIM-buh-lyz) To stand for or represent something else, such as an important event or person.

vitamin (VY-tuh-min) A substance found in foods that is needed by the body for health and growth.

Index

Websites

For web resources related to the subject of this book, go to: www.windmillbooks.com/weblinks and select this book's title.